Her Pretty Garden

BY ALYSSA KREKELBERG

Ivy has a pretty garden.
Flowers grow in
her pretty garden.

Some yellow
flowers grow in
her pretty garden.

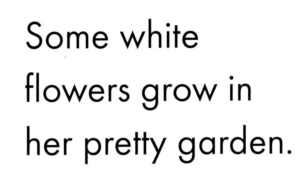

Some white
flowers grow in
her pretty garden.

Ivy waters the flowers in her pretty garden.

Ivy plants seeds in her pretty garden.

The seeds grow in her pretty garden.

There is a rabbit in her pretty garden.

There is a robin in
her pretty garden.

There is a squirrel in
her pretty garden.

The sun shines on
her pretty garden.

Note to Caregivers and Educators

Sight words are a foundation for reading. It's important for young readers to have sight words memorized at a glance without breaking them down into individual letter sounds. Sight words are often phonetically irregular and can't be sounded out, so readers need to memorize them. Knowing sight words allows readers to focus on more difficult words in the text. The intent of this book is to repeat specific sight words as many times as possible throughout the story. Through repetition of the words, emerging readers will recognize, and ideally memorize, each sight word. Memorizing sight words can help improve readers' literacy skills.

garden

her

pretty

About the Author

Alyssa Krekelberg is a children's
book editor and author. She
lives in Minnesota and enjoys
exploring the great outdoors with
her hyper husky.

Published by The Child's World®
1980 Lookout Drive • Mankato, MN 56003-1705
800-599-READ • www.childsworld.com

Photographs ©: iStockphoto, cover, 1, 2, 5, 9, 13, 21, 23; Martine
Wahlborg/iStockphoto, 6; Fang Xia Nuo/iStockphoto, 10; Cora
Mueller/iStockphoto, 14; Danita Delmont/Shutterstock Images, 17;
W. C. Johnston/iStockphoto, 18

ISBN 9781503835627
LCCN 2019943121

Printed in the United States of America